SF Bibliographies

SF Bibliographies

by
Robert E. Briney and Edward Wood

*An Annotated Bibliography
of
Bibliographical Works
on
Science Fiction
and
Fantasy Fiction*

Advent: Publishers, Inc.

Chicago: 1972

*Dedicated
to*
*the bibliographers of science fiction and
fantasy whose pioneering work prepared
the way for those who came later.*

Library of Congress Catalog Card Number: 72-86150

International Standard Book Number: 0-911682-19-8 (paper)

Copyright ©, 1972, by Robert E. Briney and Edward Wood

All rights in this book are reserved. It may not be used for any purpose without written authorization from the holders of these rights. Nor may the book or any part thereof be reproduced in any manner whatsoever without permission in writing, except for brief quotations embodied in critical articles and reviews. For information, address: ADVENT:PUBLISHERS, INC., Post Office Box 9228, Chicago, Illinois 60690. Manufactured in the United States of America by Malloy Lithographing, Inc., Ann Arbor, Michigan 48106.

FIRST EDITION (paperbound), August 1972

Contents

INTRODUCTION vii

I. MAGAZINE INDEXES 1

II. BIBLIOGRAPHIES OF INDIVIDUAL AUTHORS 15

III. GENERAL INDEXES AND CHECKLISTS 29

IV. FOREIGN LANGUAGE BIBLIOGRAPHIES 41

INDEX 43

Introduction

Fantasy fiction in general and science fiction in particular are among the most thoroughly documented of the specialized literary *genres*. Especially since the emergence of the fantasy and science fiction magazines in the 1920's, enthusiasts have been compiling uncounted indexes, checklists and bibliographies, covering the works of favorite authors, the contents of individual magazines or groups of magazines, stories centering about a common theme (utopias, future wars, the Cthulhu Mythos, etc.), or the products of various specialist publishing houses, in addition to a few more wide-ranging and comprehensive listings. Most of these projects were undertaken by the compilers for their own use or enjoyment (constructing bibliographies can be as insidiously habit-forming as collecting and reading the actual books and magazines!). The results were published in severely limited editions, using those means of reproduction dictated by convenience or finances. They were advertised mainly by word-of-mouth or by small notices in specialist publications, and were distributed principally to other collectors and fans. The percentage of these lists that found their way into libraries, to be preserved for the use of future workers, was dismayingly small.

Nowadays the picture is brighter. Academic interest in science fiction and fantasy has grown rapidly in recent years. Reference collections in the field are maintained at several universities; and as this is being written, a Science Fiction Research Association has just emerged from the planning stages. It is an appropriate time to take stock of previous bibliographic work in the field, and we hope that the present compilation will contribute toward that end.

With at most a half dozen exceptions, the works listed in this bibliography have been examined by one or both of the compilers. Many of them are in our personal libraries, and have been used over a period of years.

There are, of course, gaps in the listing presented here. Some of them are even intentional. For example, when an early work has been superseded by a later, more complete version, the latter has been given preference in the listing. Also, we have in general restricted attention to works which are primarily bibliographical in nature or intent, and deal with science fiction or fantasy as printed prose; critical analyses, biographies, and nostalgic commentaries have been excluded, as have works dealing primarily with artwork, "fanzines" (the amateur magazines of the science fiction fan world), films, radio, television, comic strips and comic books.

Finally, we have dealt almost exclusively with bibliographies which were published as separate books or pamphlets; we have not attempted to include the numerous items of this type published in the professional and amateur science fiction magazines. Much work remains to be done in recording this magazine material.

No addresses have been supplied for the individual entries. These data change too frequently, and in any case the majority of the items listed here are out of print and no longer available. However, new bibliographical works continue to appear at a steady rate. The annual *Index to the Science Fiction Magazines*, published by the New England Science Fiction Association, is one of the most useful; information on this can be obtained from

        NESFA, Inc.
        Box G, M.I.T. Branch P.O.
        Cambridge, Massachusetts 02139.

INTRODUCTION

Many of the current bibliographical works in science fiction produced in the United States are available from

        F. and S. F. Book Co.
        P.O. Box 415
        Staten Island, New York 10302.

The British counterparts can sometimes be obtained from

        Fantast (Medway) Ltd.
        39 West Street
        Wisbech, Cambs,
        England PE13 2LX

The compilers wish to thank Robert Galbreath for advice and encouragement, in addition to the more specific contribution noted in Part III of this listing.

Robert E. Briney

Salem, Massachusetts

Edward Wood

Hartford, Connecticut

May 1972

NOTE ON FORMAT:

In Parts I, III, and IV, entries are listed alphabetically by title. Entries in Part II are arranged alphabetically according to the name of the author who is the subject of the entry; some "omnibus" author checklists covering more than one author are listed at the beginning of this section.

In each entry, title and name of author or compiler are given first, followed by publication data in this order: publisher, place of publication, date of publication, pagination, size, method of reproduction, style of binding or cover, and price.

A pagination listing such as "iv-viii + 3-75 pp." means that there is front-matter on pages iv through viii, while the text begins on page 3 and runs through page 75. Only those pages that actually contain textual material are cited. Fly-leaves, title pages, copyright pages, dedication pages, etc., are not numbered in the citations.

I. Magazine Indexes

ASTOUNDING **STORY-KEY, 1920–1951,** by D. W. [Redd] Boggs (compiler, Minneapolis, Feb 1952, i + 1-18 pp., quarto, mimeo).

An alphabetical listing of the stories in *Astounding Stories* and *Astounding Science Fiction* through December 1951. In quoting titles, initial articles (A, An, The) are omitted; authors are identified by last name only; there is no cross index.

AUSTRALIAN SCIENCE FICTION INDEX, 1925–1967, compiled by Graham Stone (Australian Science Fiction Association, Canberra City, 1968, v-vi + 1-158 pp., half-legal size, mimeo, bound in heavy card covers, $3.00 Aust.).

This index covers all of the science fiction and fantasy published in magazines, paperbacks, and hard-cover books in Australia in the period 1925-1967. Magazine contents are cross-indexed by author and by story title. Brief notes on the various magazines and paperback series are included.

An earlier version was published by the Futurian Society of Sydney in 1964 covering the years 1939-1962 and containing 113 pages.

AUTHENTIC SCIENCE FICTION, compiled by Brian Burgess (probably published by the compiler; no place, date, or price given; 25-57 pp., quarto, mimeo).

A checklist of the contents of *Authentic Science Fiction* magazine, by issue, by author, and by story title. It was included in a mailing of OMPA (an amateur press association).

A CHECKLIST OF *ASTOUNDING*, by B. T(erry) Jeeves (compiler, Sheffield [England], 1963, 1965, 1970, quarto, mimeo, stapled in card covers, no price given).
    Part 1. 1930 to 1939   5-52 pp.
    Part 2. 1940 to 1949   5-45 pp.
    Part 3. 1950 to 1959

The contents of *Astounding Stories* and *Astounding Science Fiction* for the indicated years are listed by issue, by author, and by story title. There are separate lists of fact articles and "Probability Zero" features. Cover artists are identified in Parts 2 and 3, but not in Part 1. Interior artists are given in Part 3.

A CHECKLIST OF *SCIENCE FICTION ADVENTURES* (BRITISH EDITION), compiled by Roger G. Peyton (no publisher, place, or date given, 1-13 pp. [not numbered], quarto, mimeo, stapled in paper covers).

An issue-by-issue checklist, together with indexes by author and by story title.

A CHECKLIST OF *VENTURE SCIENCE FICTION* MAGAZINE, compiled by Gerald Bishop (Aardvark House, Exeter [England], 1970, 1-28 pp., [not numbered], quarto, mimeo, stapled in paper covers, 2/6 [30¢]).

The full title of this publication is *Venture Science Fiction Magazine: A Checklist of the First American Series and the British Reprint Series, With an Index to Both of These by Author and Title. Also an Index of the First Three Issues of the Second American Series.* This says it all. The checklist of the First American Series is reprinted from an earlier compilation by Bob Leman.

THE COMPLETE CHECKLIST OF SCIENCE-FICTION MAGAZINES, by Bradford M. Day (Science-Fiction and Fantasy Publications, Woodhaven [N.Y.], 1961, 3-63 pp., octavo, offset, no price given [$1.50]).

Both more and less extensive than the title indicates. The checklist gives cover dates and volume and number for all of the science fiction and fantasy magazines, as well as dozens of related or borderline magazines, covering the period from 1895 to 1960. There is no information on the contents, but the checklist tells exactly what issues were published, and when. In spite of errors and omissions (some of which were corrected in a six-page supplement issued in 1964), the checklist is extremely useful. It is the *only* reference work of its kind.

This checklist was originally made available as a 23-page mimeographed booklet; a corrected version was included in *An Index on the Weird & Fantastica in Magazines* (q.v.). The booklet here listed is considerably expanded from these earlier versions.

THE *DESTINY* INDEX OF FANTASY—1953, compiled by Edward Wood and Earl Kemp (Chicago, 1954, 1-64 pp., octavo, offset, 35¢).

This was the Fall 1954 issue of *Destiny*, an amateur magazine edited by Earl Kemp and Malcolm Willits. Pages 5-40 contain lists of the contents of all U.S. and British science fiction and fantasy magazines published during 1953. Information on illustrators, lengths of stories, and sources of reprinted material is included. Pages 41-46 contain a checklist of science fiction and fantasy books (both hardcover and paperback) published during 1953. The remainder of the issue consists of "White Paper: 1953-1954," an article by Edward Wood containing much statistical information on the growth and development of the science fiction magazines.

EVOLUTION OF MODERN SCIENCE FICTION, by Hugo Gernsback (author, New York, Aug 1952, 1-12 pp., octavo, offset).

Brief article by Gernsback, plus index (compiled by Theodore Engel) of science fiction stories in the following magazines during the period 1911-1928: *Modern Electrics, Electrical Experimenter, Science and Invention, Radio News, Practical Electrics, The Experi-*

menter. The booklet was distributed free to attenders of the World Science Fiction Convention in Chicago, 1952.

FANTASTIC NOVELS: **A CHECK LIST**, by Roger Dard, foreword by August Derleth (Dragon Press, Perth [Western Australia], 1957, printed booklet, pages not numbered, 2/6).
    A chronological listing of the contents of *Fantastic Novels* magazine.

FRED COOK'S INDEX TO THE WONDER GROUP, compiled by Frederick S. Cook (compiler, Grand Haven [Mich.], 1966, 6-239 pp., quarto, offset, stapled in heavy card covers, no price given).
    The 'Wonder Group' consisted of the pulp magazines
    Air Wonder Stories
    Captain Future
    Fantastic Story Magazine
    Fantastic Story Quarterly
    Science Wonder Quarterly
    Science Wonder Stories
    Space Stories
    Startling Stories
    Thrilling Wonder Stories
    Wonder Stories
    Wonder Stories Annual
    Wonder Stories Quarterly
published at various times between June 1929 and Fall 1955. The contents of each issue of each of these magazines are listed, and are cross-indexed by author both for individual years and for the entire run of each magazine. An outline history of each magazine is also provided.

GALAXY **CHECKLIST**. (Published by the British Science Fiction Association [no compiler, date, or price given], 1-60 pp., quarto, mimeo, stapled in paper covers; cover design by Eddie Jones.)
    The contents of *Galaxy Magazine* from Oct 1950 through Dec 1958 are listed by issue, by author, and by story title.

MAGAZINE INDEXES

A HISTORY AND CHECKLIST OF *NEW WORLDS*, compiled by Brian Burgess (British Science Fiction Association, 1959, 3-33 pp., quarto, mimeo, 2/6).

The contents of the first 55 issues of *New Worlds* (1946 through Jan 1957) are indexed by issue, by story title, and by author. An article, "A History of *New Worlds*," by John Carnell, is also included.

INDEX OF SCIENCE FICTION, compiled by William H. Evans (Robert C. Peterson, Denver [Colo.], 1949, no pagination, quarto, mimeo [one side of paper], loose sheets, sold at 30¢ per part or $1.00 for all four parts).

This pioneering work indexes the science fiction magazines of the period 1926-1948 on an issue by issue basis. The Speer Decimal Classification is used to indicate the subject matter of each story, and a three-letter code (for which no key is supplied) tries to identify the illustrator of each story. Contents of the four parts are as follows:

Part 1: *Amazing Stories*, 1926-1948.

Part 2: *Astounding Stories*, 1930-1938, and *Astounding Science Fiction*, 1938-1947.

Part 3: *Wonder Stories/Thrilling Wonder Stories*, and other "Wonder" magazines, 1929-1948.

Part 4: *Comet; Captain Future; Miracle Science and Fantasy Stories; Amazing Stories Annual; Amazing Stories Quarterly; Uncanny Stories; Stirring Science Stories; Scoops* (English); *Astonishing Stories; Planet Stories* (to Winter 1948); *Science Fiction* (first series); *Future Fiction* (first series); *Science Fiction Quarterly* (first series); *Dynamic Science Stories* (first series); *Marvel Science Stories* (to Apr 1941); *Super Science Stories* (to May 1943); *Famous Fantastic Mysteries* (to Aug 1948); *Fantastic Novels* (to Sep 1948); *Startling Stories* (to Nov 1947).

THE INDEX OF SCIENCE FICTION MAGAZINES, 1951–1965, compiled by Norm Metcalf (J. Ben Stark, Publisher, El Cerrito [Calif.], 1968, ix-xi + 1-253 pp., quarto, offset, bound in heavy paper covers, cover drawing by Vaughn Bodé, no price given [$8.50]).

The English-language science fiction magazines, as well as some of the fantasy magazines, for the period 1951-1965 are indexed by author and by story title. A separate checklist of magazines indexed provides information on size, number of pages, and cover artists. An index of editors is also included. The listing by author gives the approximate wordage of each story, plus much information on pen names and on series of connected stories.

In some respects the coverage is inconsistent: e.g., *Magazine of Horror* is indexed, but *Weird Tales* is not. In a work of this magnitude, errors (typographical and otherwise) are inevitable, but here their number seems to have been minimized. The type-face is minute, but readable.

[AN INDEX OF VARIOUS FANTASY PUBLICATIONS], compiled by Darrell C. Richardson (compiler, 1947-48, no pagination, quarto, mimeo, loose pages).

The Richardson indexes were loose-leaf pages distributed to members of the National Fantasy Fan Federation. Title sheets were issued, but no table of contents. The following indexes are known to have been circulated:
Famous Fantastic Mysteries (to 1946)
Science Fiction (1939-1941)
The Witch's Tales
Future Fiction (1939-1941)
Future Combined With Science Fiction (1941-1943)
Cosmic Stories
Science Fiction Quarterly
Marvel Science Stories, *Marvel Tales,* and *Marvel Stories* (1938-1941)
Fantasy (British)
Eerie Tales
Red Star Adventures
Uncanny Stories
Stirring Science Stories
Fantasy: The Magazine of Science Fiction
Outlands
Astonishing Stories
Golden Fleece
Fantastic Adventures (1939-1946)

[INDEX OF WEIRD—FANTASY MAGAZINES], compiled by William H. Evans (Robert C. Peterson, Denver [Colo.], 1950, 1-85 pp. [unnumbered], quarto, mimeo [one side of paper], loose sheets, no price given [$1.00]).
The index had no formal title. It contains issue by issue contents listings for *Weird Tales* (through Nov 1948), *Fantastic Adventures* (through May 1947), *Unknown, From Unknown Worlds, Witch's Tales, Oriental Stories* and *Magic Carpet, Strange Tales, Strange Stories, Unusual Stories,* and *Marvel Tales.* Occasional issues are missing from the list, and the inevitable typographical errors are present.
This index would be largely superseded by the *Index on the Weird & Fantastica in Magazines* (q.v.) if it were not for two special features. First, an attempt has been made to identify the illustrator of each story. Three-letter abbreviations are used, but since no key to the abbreviations is provided, some outside knowledge is necessary in order to decipher them. Second, and more important, the "Speer Decimal Classification" has been used to indicate the subject matter of each story (e.g., vampires, a lost race, deals with the devil). This is a very useful feature which is missing from almost all other indexes in the field. It is worthy of revival.

AN INDEX ON THE WEIRD & FANTASTICA IN MAGAZINES, (Bradford M. Day, S. Ozone Park [N.Y.], 1953, ii + iv + 1-162 pp., quarto, mimeo, stapled in heavy paper covers, $2.00). Edition limited to 400 numbered copies.
The major part of this index, pages 1-86, consists of a listing of the contents, issue by issue, of *Weird Tales* (through Nov 1953), *Golden Fleece, Strange Tales, Oriental Stories* and *Magic Carpet, Tales of Magic and Mystery, The Thrill Book,* and *Strange Stories.* With the exception of the entries for *Golden Fleece* and for *Weird Tales* 1939-1953, which were compiled by Bradford M. Day, the lists are reprinted from the *Weird Tales Index* compiled by William H. Evans and published by Julius Unger in 1942.
Pages 87-117 contain lists of the fantasy stories from *Complete Stories, Romance Magazine, Popular Magazine, The Idler, Blue Book,* and eight Frank A. Munsey publications: *All-American Fiction, All-Story Magazine, The Argosy, The Cavalier, Live Wire, Munsey's Magazine, Ocean,* and *Scrap Book.* These lists were compiled by William

H. Evans, and originally appeared in the amateur magazine *Fantasy Commentator*, 1944-1952.

There are also three pages of fragmentary listings of fantasy stories from *Adventure*, *Everybody's Magazine*, *Top Notch*, *Thrilling Adventures*, and other magazines.

Pages 121-160 consist of a "Checklist of Fantastic Magazines" by date, volume, and number. An expanded version of this checklist was published as a separate booklet; see *The Complete Checklist of Science-Fiction Magazines*.

In the story listings, authors' first names are not given, only the initials. Typographical errors are numerous throughout. Nevertheless, this is an important and useful publication. It is now quite rare.

AN INDEX TO *ANALOG* (January 1960 to June 1965), compiled by Robert Weinberg (no publisher, place, or date given; 10 pp. [not numbered], quarto, mimeo, 50¢).

An index by issue and by author. No cross-index by story title. Cover artists and series stories are listed.

INDEX TO BRITISH SCIENCE FICTION MAGAZINES, 1934–1953, [no compiler listed] (Australian Science Fiction Association, Canberra City, half-legal size, mimeo, bound in heavy card covers).

Part I: Pages 1-19 + A1-A17, no date, no price given
Part II: Pages 19-54 + B1-B30, 1968, 45¢ (Aust.)
Part III: Pages 55-91 + C1-C36, 1968, 60¢ (Aust.)

Part I lists the contents of the magazines *Scoops*, *Tales of Wonder*, and *Fantasy*. Part II covers the British edition of *Astounding Science Fiction* from Aug 1939 to Dec 1953. Part III lists the contents of *New Worlds* Nos. 1-21, *Science-Fantasy* Nos. 1-6, *Strange Tales* (British), *Thrilling Stories*, the British editions of *Science Fiction*, *Future Fiction*, *Science Fiction Quarterly*, and *Dynamic Science Fiction*, and miscellaneous compilations from the U.S. editions of these magazines.

Capsule histories of the individual magazines are given, and each of the three parts of the *Index* is cross-indexed by author, though not by story title.

INDEX TO FICTION IN *RADIO NEWS* AND OTHER MAGAZINES, compiled by T. G. L. Cockcroft (compiler, Lower Hutt [N.Z.], 1970, 1-12 pp., large octavo, offset, paper covers, no price given). Edition limited to 249 copies.

Contains indexes by author and by title of the fiction from *Radio News*, *Modern Electrics*, *Practical Electrics*, *The Experimenter*, *The Electrical Experimenter*, and *Science and Invention*. Supplementary notes, including a checklist of serials, are included.

AN INDEX TO THE BRITISH EDITIONS OF *THE MAGAZINE OF FANTASY AND SCIENCE FICTION*, with a cross-reference to the Original American Edition, compiled by A. J. L. Durie (compiler, Windlesham, Surrey [England], 1965, 1-44 pp., quarto, mimeo, stapled in paper covers, 6/-).

The British editions of *The Magazine of Fantasy and Science Fiction* were not simply reprints of corresponding U.S. issues. Each issue of the British magazine consisted of selections from several issues of the U.S. edition. This index lists the contents of each issue of the British First Series (Oct 1953—Sep 1954) and Second Series (Dec 1959—June 1964). The date of U.S. publication of each story is given, and there are cross-indexes by author and by story title.

INDEX TO THE SCIENCE FICTION MAGAZINES, 1926—1950, compiled and arranged by Donald B. Day (Perri Press, Portland [Ore.], 1952, ix-xv + 1-184 pp., quarto, offset, boards, dust jacket by Donald B. Day, $6.50 [later $8.50]). Edition of 2000 copies, bound in lots of 500 copies at a time.

The contents of approximately fifty science fiction specialty magazines, from their first issues through Dec 1950, are indexed by author and by story title. Information on pseudonyms and on sequels and series is included. A separate checklist of magazines indexed gives volume and number, page size, number of pages, and cover artist for each issue indexed.

The weird fiction magazines, such as *Weird Tales*, *Strange Tales*, and *Oriental Stories*, are not included, although such "half-and-half" magazines as *Avon Fantasy Reader* and *Unknown Worlds* are present.

This was a pioneering work which has never been superseded, and is not likely to be in the near future. It was the first of the really ambitious indexing projects, and showed that it was possible to bring order to an enormous mass of information. The entries in this index were transcribed from approximately 20,000 index cards, which in turn had been prepared from the original magazines, over a period of fifteen years. Almost all later magazine indexes in the sf field have used this index as a jumping-off place and as a model.

INDEX TO THE SCIENCE FICTION MAGAZINES: 1961, compiled by Al Lewis (compiler, Los Angeles, 1962 [1st edition], Sep 1963 [2nd edition], i + 1-41 pp., quarto, mimeo, stapled in paper covers, cover design by Don Simpson, 60¢).
INDEX TO THE SCIENCE FICTION MAGAZINES: 1962, compiled by Al Lewis with the assistance of Fred Patten and Ed Meskys (compiler, Los Angeles, Aug. 1963, i-ii + 1-54 pp., quarto, mimeo, stapled in paper covers, cover design by E. Loring Ware, 75¢).
INDEX TO THE SCIENCE FICTION AND FANTASY MAGAZINES: 1963, compiled by Al Lewis (compiler, Los Angeles, June 1964, i-ii + 1-62 pp., quarto, mimeo, stapled in paper covers, cover design by Joni Stopa, 75¢).

These were designed as supplements to Donald B. Day's *Index to the Science Fiction Magazines, 1926-1950* (q.v.). The issues for the appropriate year are listed by magazine table of contents, and cross-indexed by author and by story title. Illustrators and page numbers are listed, as well as information on pseudonyms and on sequels and series. The 1962 index contains an "Index to Book Reviews" compiled by Edmund R. Meskys, and that for 1963 contains a similar index compiled by Piers A. Jacob.

Most, but not all, of the information in these indexes is included in the two 1951-1965 indexes (MITSFS and Norm Metcalf). However, the high level of legibility, attractiveness, and accuracy of the three Lewis indexes makes them still useful and worth owning.

INDEX TO THE SCIENCE FICTION MAGAZINES, 1966, compiled by Anthony R. Lewis (New England Science Fiction Association, Cambridge [Mass.], i-ii + 1-17 pp., cover by Steve Fabian, $1.00).
INDEX TO THE SCIENCE FICTION MAGAZINES, 1967, compiled

MAGAZINE INDEXES 11

by Anthony R. Lewis (New England Science Fiction Association, Cambridge [Mass.], i-ii + 1-16 pp., cover by Steve Fabian, $1.00).
INDEX TO THE SCIENCE FICTION MAGAZINES, 1968, compiled by Anthony R. Lewis (New England Science Fiction Association, Cambridge [Mass.], i-ii + 1-17 pp., cover by Jack Gaughan, $1.00).
INDEX TO THE SCIENCE FICTION MAGAZINES, 1969, compiled by Anthony R. Lewis (New England Science Fiction Association, Cambridge [Mass.], i-ii + 1-20 pp., cover by George Barr, $1.00).
INDEX TO THE SCIENCE FICTION MAGAZINES, 1966–1970, compiled by Anthony R. Lewis (New England Science Fiction Association, Cambridge [Mass.], August 1971, vii-ix + 1-82 pp., quarto, offset, hardbound, $5.00).

The first four are the annual supplements to the *MIT Science Fiction Society's Index to the S-F Magazines, 1951-1965* (q.v.), the distribution of which has been taken over by the New England Science Fiction Association, Inc. The 1967 to 1969 indexes were published early in the year following the cover date. An early version of the 1966 index was compiled by Erwin S. Strauss and published in 1967 in a crudely mimeographed format. When this version went out of print, the 1966 index was re-compiled by A. R. Lewis and published in 1969 in a format matching the other supplements. The five-year index is in the same format, but has been bound in permanent hardcover form. The text was offset from a computer printout.

INDEX TO THE VERSE IN *WEIRD TALES*, compiled by Thomas G. L. Cockcroft (compiler, Lower Hutt [New Zealand], Dec 1960, 3-17 pp., octavo, offset, no price given, 500-copy edition).

The verse in *Weird Tales*, *Oriental Stories*, *The Magic Carpet Magazine*, and *The Thrill Book* is cross-indexed by title and by author.

INDEX TO THE WEIRD FICTION MAGAZINES, compiled by T. G. L. Cockcroft (compiler, Lower Hutt [N.Z.], 1962 and 1964, 5-57 and 58-101 pp., large octavo, offset, stapled in heavy card covers).

Published in two parts. The *Index by Title* was published in Nov 1962. It lists, alphabetically by title, all stories in the following magazines: *Strange Stories*, *Strange Tales*, *The Thrill Book*, *Oriental Stories*, *The Magic Carpet Magazine*, *Strange Tales* (British), *Golden*

Fleece, and *Weird Tales.*

Additional checklists, covering such information as cover artists, pseudonyms, pictorial features, and serials, are included. The *Index by Author,* covering the same magazines, was published in Sep 1964, priced at $2.75.

AN INDEX TO *UNKNOWN* AND *UNKNOWN WORLDS* BY AUTHOR AND BY TITLE, compiled by Stuart Hoffman (The Sirius Press, Black Earth [Wis.], 1955, i-ii + 1-34 pp. plus Addenda sheet, quarto, printed, spiral bound in stiff cardboard covers, no price given [$1.00]).

The contents of *Unknown* and *Unknown Worlds* are listed by author and by story title. The index by title includes notes on the locale and principal characters in each story, and there is a separate alphabetical checklist of principal characters. The Addenda sheet contains a checklist of volume number, issue number, and date for each magazine. The booklet also contains a two-page preface, "Persons Unknown," by Robert Bloch.

JOURNAL OF SCIENCE FICTION 1951 MAGAZINE INDEX, by Edward Wood (Chicago, 1952, 3-32 pp., octavo, offset, 25¢).

This was volume 1, number 3 of the amateur magazine *Journal of Science Fiction,* edited by Charles Freudenthal and Edward Wood. The entire issue was devoted to lists of the contents of all science fiction and fantasy magazines published in the U.S. and Britain during 1951. Information on illustrators, lengths of stories, and sources of reprinted material was also given.

JOURNAL OF SCIENCE FICTION 1952 MAGAZINE INDEX, by Edward Wood (Chicago, 1953, 49-80 pp., octavo, offset, 50¢).

This was bound together with volume 1, number 4 of the amateur magazine *Journal of Science Fiction.* Magazine coverage is as described in the entry above. Also of interest is a checklist of articles about science fiction, 1925-1952, transcribed by Edward Wood from the *Reader's Guide to Periodical Literature.* For continuation, see *The Destiny Index of Fantasy—1953.*

THE MIT SCIENCE FICTION SOCIETY'S INDEX TO THE S-F MAGAZINES, 1951–1965, compiled by Erwin S. Strauss (MIT Science Fiction Society, Cambridge [Mass.], 1966, i-ii + 1-207 pp., quarto, offset, boards, no price given [$8.00]).

Contents of all English-language fantasy and science fiction magazines for the years 1951-1965 are listed by magazine, by story title, and by author. A separate checklist (compiled by Anthony R. Lewis) gives the volume number, issue number, cover date, size, number of pages, and cover artist for all issues indexed. No information on illustrators, pen names, or series is included.

The entries for this index were keypunched on IBM cards and the listings were compiled by computer. The final index was printed by photo-offset from the computer print-out. The type-face is small but legible, entirely in upper-case letters.

A preliminary version of this index, covering only six magazines, was issued in mimeographed form under the title *The Bluedex/Blackdex*, priced at $2.00.

Annual supplements to this index are issued: see *Index to the Science Fiction Magazines* 1966 et seq.

NEBULA: **AN INDEX**, compiled by Maxim Jakubowski (British Science Fiction Association, 1963, 2-18 pp. [not numbered], legal size, mimeo, stapled, no price given).

Preface by Brian W. Aldiss, introduction by E. C. Tubb.

An index to the 41 issues (Autumn 1952–June 1959) of the Scottish science fiction magazine *Nebula*. Contents of each issue are listed, and there is a cross-index by author (though not by story title). The prefatory matter and a final page of miscellaneous comments constitute an appreciation and capsule history of the magazine.

II. Bibliographies of Individual Authors

AUTHOR'S WORKS LISTINGS, by Donald H. Tuck (compiler, Hobart [Tasmania], 1960-62, small quarto, mimeo, loose sheets [unbound]).
"A series of bibliographies listing the books, pocket books and stories of prominent authors together with other pertinent material."
  Series I, Feb 1960, 25¢
    Isaac Asimov (8 pp.)
    Nelson S. Bond (7 pp.) [revised, Aug 1960]
    Fredric Brown (4 pp.)
    Hal Clement (Harry Clement Stubbs) (2 pp.)
    Ray Cummings (5 pp.)
    Robert A. Heinlein (6 pp.)
    Damon Knight (3 pp.)
    Stanley G. Weinbaum (2 pp.)
  Series II, Sep 1960
    Poul Anderson (7 pp.)
    Arthur C. Clarke (10 pp.)
    David H. Keller (6 pp.)
    Otis Adelbert Kline (2 pp.)
    Murray Leinster (William Fitzgerald Jenkins) (9 pp.)
    Nathan Schachner (3 pp.)
    Henry S. Whitehead (4 pp.)

Series III, Feb 1962
    August W. Derleth (sf and fantasy only) (10 pp.)
    Edmond Hamilton (8 pp.)
    Cyril M. Kornbluth (7 pp.)
    Frank Belknap Long (7 pp.)
    Eric Frank Russell (6 pp.)
    Clifford D. Simak (5 pp.)

Further series were planned but not issued. The format is similar to that of the same compiler's *Handbook of Science Fiction and Fantasy*, q.v.

BIBLIOGRAPHY OF ADVENTURE (Mundy, Burroughs, Rohmer, Haggard), by Bradford M. Day (Science Fiction and Fantasy Publications, Denver [N.Y.], 1964, 1-125 pp., quarto, mimeo, stapled in card covers, no price given [$2.50]). Edition limited to 300 copies.

Contains revised versions of earlier bibliographies of Talbot Mundy, Sax Rohmer, and Edgar Rice Burroughs, and a detailed descriptive bibliography of H. Rider Haggard first editions.

[AN INDEX OF THE WORKS OF VARIOUS FANTASY AUTHORS], by Darrell C. Richardson (compiler, 1947-48, unpaged, loose sheets, quarto, mimeo, no price given).

This set of indexes was distributed to members of the National Fantasy Fan Federation, but apparently not all pages were sent to every member. A title page was provided, but no contents page.

Although the pages were neatly mimeographed, the format led to confusion: lists for two authors were placed on opposite sides of the same sheet, and some author lists were mixed with magazine indexes.

The following authors are known to have been covered in these indexes: John W. Campbell, Jr. (incomplete), George Allan England (incomplete), Philip M. Fisher, Jr., Homer Eon Flint, Austin Hall, William Hope Hodgson, Abraham Merritt, C. A. "Tod" Robbins, Francis Stevens, T. S. Stribling, John Taine (Eric Temple Bell), Stanley G. Weinbaum, and Arthur Leo Zagat.

In addition, an index to *Strange Tales* was included.

INDIVIDUAL AUTHORS

STELLA NOVA: The Contemporary Science Fiction Authors, compiled by Robert Reginald (Unicorn & Son, Los Angeles, 1970, unpaged, quarto, offset, spiral bound in card covers, $15.00; out of print).

This is a listing of 308 contemporary science fiction writers who responded to a questionnaire sent out by the compiler. For each writer there is autobiographical information, the first known story or book, a list of books published by year, and description of works in progress. The publication contains much valuable information, particularly biographical, but the bibliographical information is incomplete.

This booklet was prepared primarily for sale to libraries. It was not widely advertised and was not generally available through the normal sales outlets. A revised and updated edition, with wider distribution, would be a definite service to the sf field.

ITEM FORTY-THREE. BRIAN W. ALDISS: A BIBLIOGRAPHY 1954—1962, compiled by Margaret Manson, with annotations by Brian Aldiss (Dryden Press, Birmingham [England], Dec 1962, [24 pp.], octavo, printed pamphlet, no price given).

Lists Aldiss' fiction alphabetically by title, including reprints and foreign-language translations. A second list is arranged alphabetically according to the magazine or anthology in which the stories appeared. A third list covers Aldiss' non-fiction and miscellaneous writings, and a fourth gives the contents of two anthologies which he edited. Brief comments by Aldiss appear throughout the listings, as well as a "Postscript" at the end.

A CHECKLIST OF POUL ANDERSON, by Roger G. Peyton (compiler, Birmingham [England], Aug 1965, 1-26 pp., quarto, mimeo, illus., 3/6 [50¢]).

Checklist of Poul Anderson's science fiction and fantasy writing, generally complete up to the time of publication. Omits Anderson's mysteries, historical fiction, and non-fiction.

INDIVIDUAL AUTHORS

ROBERT BLOCH BIBLIOGRAPHY, compiled by Graham M. Hall (compiler, Tewksbury [England], January 1965, 3-32 pp., quarto, mimeo, stapled in paper covers, no price given).

This oddly arranged bibliography comprises two lists. The first is a listing of Bloch's professionally published work from 1935 through December 1964, in chronological order of publication: short stories and novels; sf, fantasy, and mystery; English and foreign languages, all in the same list. Each reprint, identified by an asterisk, is listed in its chronological place rather than with the original appearance of the story. Approximate length of each story is given. In a second list, the shorter works are arranged according to the magazines in which they were published. An "Addendum" provides a checklist of anthologies that have included Bloch stories; contents lists for Bloch's short-story collections; a checklist of the "Lefty Feep" series; and a list of radio, TV, and film adaptations and original scripts. The booklet also contains a foreword, "Building Bloch," by Samuel A. Peeples, and a short "Author's Note" by Bloch.

A. BOUCHER BIBLIOGRAPHY, compiled by J. R. Christopher, D. W. Dickensheet, and R. E. Briney (Allen J. Hubin, White Bear Lake [Minn.], 1969, [34 pp.], quarto, offset, no price given).

Exhaustively annotated bibliography of Boucher's writings in all fields. It is an offprint from *The Armchair Detective*, Vol. 2, Nos. 2-4, bound together with *A Boucher Portrait: Anthony Boucher as Seen by His Friends and Colleagues*, compiled by Lenore Glen Offord. The offprint was prepared for private circulation, but some extra copies were offered for sale at 75¢.

This contains much biographical and bibliographical information not available elsewhere.

RAY BRADBURY REVIEW, edited by William F. Nolan (Wm. F. Nolan, San Diego [Calif.], 1952, 5-64 pp., octavo, offset, stapled in paper covers, 50¢).

This booklet contains three articles and a story by Bradbury, an assortment of biographical and critical articles on Bradbury (by Anthony Boucher, Henry Kuttner, Chad Oliver, and others), a compi-

INDIVIDUAL AUTHORS

lation of quotations from reviews of *The Martian Chronicles* and *The Illustrated Man*, and three parodies of Bradbury's writing.

Pages 46-63 consist of "The Ray Bradbury Index," a bibliography of Bradbury's published works through December 1951. Both original and reprint appearances are included, as well as radio adaptations.

A 12-page mimeographed supplement entitled *The Ray Bradbury Index* was published in 1954. A revised and up-dated Bradbury bibliography, also compiled by William F. Nolan, was published in the May 1963 issue of *The Magazine of Fantasy and Science Fiction*.

EDGAR RICE BURROUGHS: A BIBLIOGRAPHY, by Bradford M. Day (Science-Fiction & Fantasy Publications, Woodhaven [N.Y.], 1962, 6-45 pp., large octavo, offset, heavy paper covers, cover illustration by Gilbert Kane, $1.10).

Checklist of Burroughs' books and magazine stories (7-34 pp.), a brief biographical sketch, reviews and summaries of a few selected titles, and checklists of newspaper serials, comic strips, Big Little Books, and Spanish-language Tarzan pastiches. A useful and accurate compilation.

An earlier version of this work was issued as a mimeographed pamphlet: *Edgar Rice Burroughs Biblio*, edited by Bradford M. Day (Science-Fiction and Fantasy Publications, New York, 1956, 1-28 pp., quarto, mimeo, stapled in heavy card covers, 50¢).

A GOLDEN ANNIVERSARY BIBLIOGRAPHY OF EDGAR RICE BURROUGHS, compiled and edited by Henry Hardy Heins. Complete Edition, Revised (Donald M. Grant, West Kingston [R.I.], June 1964, iv + 5-418 pp., large octavo, printed, $10.00).

The first edition was published by the compiler in September 1962: 2-123 pp., combination of mimeo and photo-offset, quarto, loose pages punched for 3-ring binder, in heavy card covers, $3.00.

The Complete Edition, Revised, was originally announced as Part II of the first edition. It was offered on advance subscription at $5.00 per copy. The edition, limited to 1000 copies, was sold out soon after publication.

The book is one of the most remarkable bibliographic volumes ever published. Pages 5-247 contain a complete bibliography of all editions of all of Burroughs' published works, exhaustively annotated and cross-indexed, together with reprints of four short articles by Burroughs. Pages 251-409 contain another Burroughs article, a checklist of the illustrators of the Burroughs books, a portfolio reproducing all the magazine illustrations by J. Allen St. John for Burroughs stories, a checklist of St. John's non-Burroughs illustrations, and a second portfolio reproducing all the publishers' display advertising for the Burroughs books for the period 1914-1963.

Periodic supplements to this work appeared in the amateur magazine *ERB-dom*, beginning in issue No. 11, Summer 1964.

THE LITERATURE OF BURROUGHSIANA, by John Harwood (Camille Cazedessus, Jr., Baton Rouge [La.], Feb 1963, ii + 6-105 pp., quarto, multilith & mimeo, stapled in card covers, cover illustration from a painting by J. Allen St. John [$2.00 after publication, but available on advance subscription for 60¢]).

Subtitled: "A listing of magazine articles, book commentaries, news items, book reviews, movie reviews, fanzines, amateur publications and related items concerning the life and/or works of Edgar Rice Burroughs."

The items listed are divided into six general categories; entries in each category are listed chronologically. Over 1000 items are listed in all, covering more than forty years of commentary on Burroughs and his works.

The booklet also contains an Introduction by Henry Hardy Heins, a Foreword by the publisher, and a ten-page Commentary by the compiler.

A JOHN CREASEY BIBLIOGRAPHY, by R. E. Briney and John Creasey (Allen J. Hubin, White Bear Lake [Minn.], 1968, [22 pp.], quarto, offset, no price given).

An offprint from *The Armchair Detective*, Vol. 2, No. 1 (Oct 1968), bound together with an article, "John Creasey—Fact or Fiction," by John Creasey. A corrected version of the bibliography was issued in 1969. Both versions were prepared for private circulation, and not offered for sale.

INDIVIDUAL AUTHORS 21

100 BOOKS BY AUGUST DERLETH, [compiled by August Derleth], with a foreword by Donald Wandrei (Arkham House, Sauk City [Wis.], 1962, 5-121 pp., small 12mo, printed chapbook, heavy paper cover, illustrated with photographs, cover design by Gary Gore, $2.00). Edition limited to 1225 copies.

Detailed bibliography of Derleth's published books in all fields through 1962, together with checklists of anthology appearances, work in progress, magazines that have published his work, and quotations from biographical sketches and critical appraisals. The bibliographical information includes complete contents listings of all of Derleth's short story and poetry collections and edited anthologies.

An earlier compilation of the same type was issued in 1951, and distributed free to mail-order patrons of Arkham House: *August Derleth: Twenty-Five Years of Writing, 1926-1951* (Arkham House, 1951, 1-24 pp., frontis., 16mo, printed chapbook, stapled in gray paper covers).

JOHN RUSSELL FEARN—AN EVALUATION, by Philip Harbottle (Coulson Publications, Wabash [Ind.], 1963, 10 pp., quarto, mimeo, no price given).

"Yandro Bibliographical Supplement #1," distributed free with the Jan 1963 issue of the amateur magazine *Yandro*; later offered for sale at 25¢.

Three-page essay plus bibliography of Fearn's science fiction in magazines, paperbacks, hardcover books, and anthologies. It was superseded by later listings: see the next two entries.

JOHN RUSSELL FEARN: THE ULTIMATE ANALYSIS, by Philip Harbottle (author, Wallsend-on-Tyne [England], 1965, 1-94 pp., [not numbered], legal size, mimeo, 4/-).

This second Fearn bibliography is much more comprehensive than either the first or the third. The thoroughness shown by the compiler in this publication makes it a model to be followed by other bibliographers.

THE MULTI-MAN. A biographic and bibliographic study of John Russell Fearn (1908-1960), by Philip Harbottle (author, Wallsend-on-Tyne [England], 1968, 1-69 pp., small quarto, offset, spiral bound in card covers, illustrated, no price given).

A biographical essay and critical evaluation (34 pp.) and an extended bibliography of Fearn's writing in all fields. The bibliography is fully annotated: comments ranging from brief plot summaries to extended analyses accompany all titles.

A BIBLIOGRAPHY OF THE WORKS OF SIR HENRY RIDER HAGGARD, 1856–1925, by J. E. Scott (Elkin Matthews Ltd., Takeley [England], 1947, 5-258 pp., octavo, $4.00). Edition of 500 copies.

A listing of the first editions of H. R. Haggard's works with much additional information such as parodies, critical articles, interviews, letters to newspapers, etc. It is said to have many errors which were corrected in periodic supplements.

HARRY HARRISON/BIBLIOGRAPHIA (1951–1965), compiled by Francesco Biamonti, with Annotations by Harry Harrison (no publisher listed, Trieste, 1965, 9 pp. [not numbered], octavo, printed booklet, no price given).

Alphabetical list of Harry Harrison's writings—stories, articles, guest editorials, and a poem—through July 1965, with brief annotations by Harrison, a two-page introduction by the compiler, and a drawing of Harrison by Rudy Cristiano. Information on reprint editions and foreign-language editions is included.

THE ROBERT E. HOWARD FANTASY BIBLIO, compiled by Robert Weinberg (Mike Deckinger & Robert Weinberg, Newark [N.J.], 1969, 1-7 pp., quarto, offset, stapled in paper covers, 50¢).

Robert E. Howard's fantasy stories are listed alphabetically by title, with original and reprint appearances cited. A second list gives the contents of all of Howard's books, and a third summarizes the four major series in his fantasy fiction. A list of collaborations and two pages of miscellaneous notes are also included.

The compilation contains a number of errors, factual as well as typographical. Its usefuness is further diminished by poor legibility. Much more extensive and accurate bibliographies of Howard's work have been published in the magazine *The Howard Collector*, edited by Glenn Lord.

ALDOUS HUXLEY: A BIBLIOGRAPHY, 1916–1959, by Claire John Eschelbach and Joyce Lee Shober (University of California Press, Berkeley & Los Angeles, 1961).

HENRY KUTTNER. A MEMORIAL SYMPOSIUM, edited by Karen Anderson (Sevagram Enterprises, Berkeley [Calif.], Aug 1958, 4-34 pp., quarto, mimeo, no price given).

Memorial articles by Karen Anderson, Poul Anderson, Fritz Leiber, Richard Matheson, Ray Bradbury, Anthony Boucher, and Robert Bloch; reprint of a short story by Kuttner; and bibliography of Kuttner's science fiction writings, compiled by Donald H. Tuck. The bibliography covers the magazine science fiction and fantasy under all pseudonyms, as well as the hardcover and paperback books; Kuttner's general pulp fiction is not included.

MURRAY LEINSTER (WILL F. JENKINS): A BIBLIOGRAPHY, compiled by Mark Owings (Washington Science Fiction Association, Washington [D.C.], 1970, 2-9 pp. [not numbered], octavo, offset, pages folded but not stapled, no price given).

This brochure was the Program Booklet for the 1970 Disclave, a conference of science fiction fans held in Washington, D.C., in May 1970. It was also distributed with the March-May 1970 issue of *The WSFA Journal*.

The bibliography is an alphabetical listing of sf stories and books by Will F. Jenkins and his pseudonyms Murray Leinster and William Fitzgerald. Reprint appearances and foreign editions are included.

H. P. LOVECRAFT: A BIBLIOGRAPHY, by Joseph Payne Brennan (Biblio Press, Washington [D.C.], 1952, revised edition, 1-14 pp., octavo, printed pamphlet, no price given).

An expansion of the earlier, privately printed *Select Bibliography of H. P. Lovecraft*. It lists Lovecraft's books, stories in professional magazines, and appearances in anthologies, and also contains brief mention of books about Lovecraft, Lovecraft's pseudonyms, etc. It is generally complete up to the time of publication, but makes no attempt to list Lovecraft's amateur press writings, non-fiction, or verse. Vast amounts of information in all these areas have come to light since the publication of this bibliography.

HOWARD PHILLIPS LOVECRAFT—MEMOIRS, CRITIQUES & BIBLIOGRAPHIES, edited by George T. Wetzel (SSR Publications, North Tonawanda [N.Y.], August 1955, 5-83 pp., quarto, mimeo, stapled in card covers, no price given). Edition of 200 copies.

Contains: six essays on Lovecraft and his works; a bibliography of Lovecraft's essays, stories, and verse in amateur press publications, compiled by George T. Wetzel; and a bibliography of Lovecraft's professionally published works, plus revisions and related fiction by other authors, compiled by Robert E. Briney. These bibliographies were based partially on earlier compilations by Joseph Payne Brennan, William H. Evans and Francis T. Laney, and T. G. L. Cockcroft; in turn, these lists were incorporated into the later Lovecraft bibliographies by Jack L. Chalker [see next entry].

The bibliographies were also issued separately as Volume VII in The Lovecraft Collector's Library, a series of mimeographed booklets; 75 numbered copies, sold by advance subscription only.

THE NEW H. P. LOVECRAFT BIBLIOGRAPHY, compiled and edited by Jack L. Chalker & Divers Hands (Anthem Press Chapbook [Chalker & Associates], Baltimore [Md.], 1962, vi + 7-40 pp., quarto, mimeo, stapled in card covers, cover design by Joe Mayhew). Edition of 110 copies, presubscribed before publication.

A bibliography of Lovecraft's appearances in professional and amateur publications and books, together with lists of revisions, asso-

INDIVIDUAL AUTHORS 25

ciated fiction by other authors, and articles and books about Lovecraft. Works in foreign languages are also covered.

An expanded and corrected version of this bibliography was published in the book *The Dark Brotherhood and Other Pieces*, by H. P. Lovecraft & Divers Hands (Arkham House, Sauk City [Wis.], 1966).

THE JDM MASTER CHECKLIST. A Bibliography of the Published Writings of John D. MacDonald, compiled and edited by Len and June Moffatt and William J. Clark (Moffatt House, Downey [Calif.], Feb 1969, vi-xvii + 1-42 pp., quarto, mimeo, $1.00).

Bibliography of MacDonald's writing in all fields, including science fiction. It has extensive data on wordage, pseudonyms, foreign editions, etc.

ARTHUR MACHEN: A BIBLIOGRAPHY, compiled by Henry Danielson (compiler, London, 1923, v-x + 1-59 pp., octavo, boards). Edition of 500 copies.

In addition to the bibliography, this small book contains autobiographical and critical notes by Machen and an introduction by Henry Savage.

A. MERRITT: A BIBLIOGRAPHY OF FANTASTIC WRITINGS, by W(alter) Jas. Wentz (George A. Bibby, Roseville [Calif.], Sep 1965, 2-33 pp., quarto, mimeo, no price given). First edition limited to 200 copies, of which 175 were offered for sale.

Complete bibliography of Merritt's writings in the areas of fantasy and science fiction, with extensive annotations and commentary. Awkward format.

TALBOT MUNDY BIBLIO. Materials Toward a Bibliography of the Works of Talbot Mundy, by Bradford M. Day (Science Fiction and Fantasy Publications, South Ozone Park [N.Y.], 1955, 1-28 pp., quarto, mimeo, stapled in card covers, no price given [50¢]). Edition of 200 copies.

Biographical sketch (2 pp.) and bibliography. Includes article and checklist (5 pp.) on Mundy's various "sagas" and series, by Dr. J. Lloyd Eaton. A revised edition is included in *Bibliography of Adventure*, q.v.

SAX ROHMER. A BIBLIOGRAPHY, by Bradford M. Day (Science Fiction and Fantasy Publications, Denver [N.Y.], 1963, 5-34 pp., quarto, mimeo, stapled in card covers, no price given [$1.25]).

Bibliography, biographical sketch, and brief article on film adaptations of Rohmer's work.

The bibliographical data is often incomplete; there are several errors (typographical and otherwise) and omissions. A revised edition is included in *Bibliography of Adventure*, q.v.

THE WORKS OF M. P. SHIEL. A Study in Bibliography, by A. Reynolds Morse (Fantasy Publishing Co., Inc., Los Angeles, 1948, xiii-xvii + 1-170 pp., octavo, boards [paperbound edition released in 1971], dust jacket design adapted by Jack Gaughan from a Salvador Dali painting, $6.00).

The edition was supposedly limited to 1000 numbered copies. However, non-numbered copies have always been plentiful, and the book was still in print in both hardcover and paperback in 1971.

The bulk of this work is taken up with meticulous descriptions of all editions of Shiel's books, with copious annotations. The collaborations with Louis Tracy under the pseudonym "Gordon Holmes" are included. Separate checklists cover short stories, articles, translations, contributions to periodicals, and unpublished manuscripts. Two Shiel essays, "About Myself" and "The Inconsistency of a Novelist," are included in the book, along with miscellaneous biographical material and the text of the address delivered by Edward Shanks at Shiel's funeral. There are 11 illustrations, including portraits of Shiel and facsimiles of manuscript pages.

THE ELECTRIC BIBLIOGRAPH, Part 1: CLIFFORD D. SIMAK, by Mark Owings (Alice & Jay Haldeman, Baltimore [Md.], 1971, unpaged, quarto, mimeo, no price given).

This listing of the stories of Clifford D. Simak is a revision of a bibliography first published in *The WSFA Journal*, No. 66, April-May 1969. It lists original appearances, reprints, title changes, and foreign editions. (Not all bibliographical information is included for all editions.) An excellent production, and only one of an extended series which all deserve publication in more permanent form, by one of the best of present-day sf bibliographers.

THE TALES OF CLARK ASHTON SMITH. A BIBLIOGRAPHY, by Thomas G. L. Cockcroft (compiler, Lower Hutt [New Zealand], Nov 1951, i-v pp., large octavo, printed pamphlet, no price given). Edition of 500 copies.

Alphabetical checklist of the stories of Clark Ashton Smith, including both original and reprint appearances, with separate lists of Smith's anthology appearances and collections.

A 2-page addenda sheet, offset, was published in September 1959.

H. G. WELLS: A COMPREHENSIVE BIBLIOGRAPHY, compiled and published by The H. G. Wells Society (distributed by Michael Katanka [Books] Ltd., Edgware [Middlesex, England], 1968, v + 1-69 pp., octavo, boards).

First published in 1966; revised edition, 1968. Foreword by Kingsley Martin.

This lists Wells' books, short stories, and miscellaneous writings, including book prefaces; it also covers film and stage adaptations, and some articles about Wells. A brief biographical outline is also included.

III. General Indexes and Checklists

ARKHAM HOUSE: THE FIRST 20 YEARS, 1939–1959. A History and Bibliography, prepared by August Derleth (Arkham House, Sauk City [Wis.], 1959, i-liv pp., small 12mo, printed chapbook, heavy paper covers, cover design by Frank Utpatel, $1.00).

Edition limited to 801 copies; 80 copies were hard-bound and distributed almost exclusively to libraries.

Contains a 14-page article on the history of Arkham House, and a complete bibliography of all books published by Arkham House and the associated imprints of Mycroft & Moran and Stanton & Lee through 1959.

Note: Through the years, Arkham House has issued a number of stock lists and catalogues of its books, in the form of small printed pamphlets, 16mo size, distributed free to mail-order patrons. These pamphlets have contained much interesting biographical and bibliographical material on the authors of Arkham House books.

See also *Thirty Years of Arkham House*.

BRITISH SCIENCE FICTION BOOK INDEX 1955, compiled by Kenneth F. Slater (Fantast [Medway] Ltd., Wisbech [England], nd [1956], 2-14 pp., quarto, mimeo, stapled in heavy paper covers, no price given). Limited to 160 numbered copies.

Checklist of science fiction and fantasy books, both hardcover and paperback, published in Britain in 1955. The main list is arranged alphabetically by author and cross-indexed by title.

CHECKLIST OF ACE S-F THROUGH 1968, compiled by Marty Massoglia (East Lansing [Michigan], 1969, 1-11 pp. [unnumbered], mimeo, legal size, stapled at top, 25¢).

A checklist of science fiction titles published by Ace Publishing Corporation (Ace Books), arranged chronologically by publisher's stock number. No cross-index by author or title.

Despite errors and omissions, the checklist is useful as a summary of one publisher's contribution to the sf field.

A CHECKLIST OF ANTHOLOGIES: A title listing of science-fiction, fantasy, and weird anthologies, by Donald H. Tuck (compiler, Lindisfarne [Tasmania], Aug 1959, i-ii + 1-28 pp., small quarto, mimeo, 40¢).

Checklist of titles of science fiction anthologies, cross-indexed by editor. It gives publisher, date, pagination, and price, but does *not* list the contents of the anthologies. It covers both U.S. and British books, both hardcover and paperback. A "Supplementary Listing" (4 pp.) covers mystery anthologies and other miscellaneous collections whose contents are only partially sf or fantasy.

THE CHECKLIST OF FANTASTIC LITERATURE. A Bibliography of Fantasy, Weird, and Science Fiction Books Published in the English Language, edited by Everett F. Bleiler (Shasta Publishers, Chicago, 1948, vii-xvii + 3-455 pp., 12mo, dust jacket by Hannes Bok, $6.00).

The main index is by author, cross indexed by title. There is also an annotated list of critical and historical reference works, a list of associational items, and several pages of notes. Ever since its publication this has been the basic bibliographic reference work on fantastic literature in the English language since 1764. Its listings include novels, collections of short stories, and anthologies. Non-prose works (poetry and plays) are excluded, as are books of mythology, folklore, fairy tales, and 'true' stories of supernatural or psychic phenomena. Inevitably, there are many gaps in the listings, and many non-fantasy titles are included by mistake. In spite of such defects, this pioneering work is still eminently useful.

THE CHECKLIST OF FANTASTIC LITERATURE IN PAPERBOUND BOOKS, compiled by Bradford M. Day (Science-Fiction & Fantasy Publications, Denver [N.Y.], 1965, i + 1-128 pp., quarto, mimeo, stapled in heavy paper covers, $6.00).

According to the compiler, this checklist represents "a listing of paper-covered books with a sufficient tinge of the super-natural, or, the super-scientific as to warrant placement in the science-fantasy field." Nominally, the coverage extends to all English-language paperbound publications, including Canadian, British, and Australian, and ranges in date from the 19th century to early 1965. In actuality, only one paperbound edition is listed for each title. Usually this is the first paperbound publication of that title, but not invariably so. Publishers' stock numbers are not given, and the dates listed are not always accurate, so it is often not possible to determine which edition is being listed. In identifying publishers, the compiler makes no distinction between Gold Medal and Crest books (recording Fawcett in both cases); similarly, Pocket Books, Cardinal Editions, and Permabooks are all listed as Pocket Books; and no distinction is made between early U.S. Penguin editions (later Signet) and the British Penguin editions. In addition to a variety of minor errors, a few non-existent editions are recorded. (For example, there was no paperback called *Slaves of Sumuru* by Sax Rohmer in 1952.) On the other hand, some authors of importance are omitted altogether: Edward Bellamy, Anthony Burgess, Daphne du Maurier, Robert Graves, Eric Hatch, and J. B. Priestley. [Robert Galbreath]

A CHECKLIST OF SCIENCE FICTION ANTHOLOGIES, compiled by W(alter) R. Cole. Introduction by Theodore Sturgeon. (Compiler, Brooklyn [N.Y.], 1964, v-xvi + 1-374 pp., quarto, offset, boards, dust jacket by Tim Dumont, $7.50).

This compilation lists the contents of some 260 anthologies of science fiction and fantasy published in the English language since

1927. There are four lists: by anthology title, by editor's name, by story title, and by author's name. (The listings for the years 1962-63 are in a separate supplement, added after the bulk of the work had been done.) Full bibliographic citations are given for each anthology, and the original source of each story has been indicated, wherever possible.

This is an invaluable reference for casual readers, collectors, librarians (and future anthologists!). There is only one comment on the debit side: the book was offset printed from masters typed in a hard-to-read sans-serif typeface, and with an unevenly inked ribbon, making the result rather hard on the eyes.

A CHECKLIST OF SCIENCE FICTION, FANTASY, AND SUPERNATURAL STORIES AVAILABLE IN PAPERBACK IN BRITAIN —January 1966, compiled by Kenneth F. Slater (Fantast [Medway] Ltd., Wisbech [England], Jan 1966, 1-30 pp., legal size, mimeo, 7/6 [$1.00]).

The title indicates the scope of the checklist. It is heavily annotated with plot summaries, lists of contents for anthologies and collections, and occasional information on earlier editions of books.

It was prepared primarily as a stock-list for the booksellers Fantast (Medway) Ltd. Addenda sheets to keep the list up to date were issued periodically during 1966 and 1967.

THE DUKE UNIVERSITY UTOPIA COLLECTION, by Glenn R. Negley (Friends of Duke University Library, Durham [N.C.], 1965).

THE EDWARD WOOD—EARL KEMP INDEX OF PAPERBOUND SCIENCE FANTASY, 1938—19— (Earl Kemp, Chicago, 1959-1960, 3-52 pp., quarto, mimeo).

Three installments of this index were issued: Ace Books (pp. 5-17, coverage through mid-October 1959); Avon Books (pp. 19-32, coverage through December 1959); Ballantine Books (pp. 33-52, coverage through December 1959). Each installment consists of a chronological list of titles, arranged according to publisher's stock number, with a cross-index by author. Original sources of reprinted material are given in many cases. The installments were distributed to members of the Spectator Amateur Press Society, and were not offered for sale.

The complete index, covering all publishers, was compiled with the assistance of many fans and collectors. It was to have been published by Advent, but through circumstances beyond the control of either compilers or publishers, the only existing manuscript was lost.

A HANDBOOK OF SCIENCE FICTION AND FANTASY, compiled by Donald H. Tuck. Second Edition, Revised and Enlarged. (Compiler, Hobart [Tasmania], April 1959, vii-ix + 1-184 + 185-296 pp., legal size, mimeo, bound in blue card covers, $6.75.)

In two volumes:
   Part 1: Introduction and Main Text, A—L
   Part 2: Main Text, M—Z; and Appendices

Subtitled: "A collection of material acting as a bibliographic survey to the fields of science fiction and fantasy (including weird), covering the magazines, books, pocket books, personalities, etc., of these fields up to December 1957."

This is a remarkable work, which more than lives up to its subtitle. It includes biographical sketches of authors, bibliographies of individual authors' works in sf and fantasy, complete lists of contents of short-story collections and anthologies, plus data on sf artists, magazines, and movies. There are separate checklists of magazine issues, pseudonyms, connected stories and sequels, and paperback books.

The first edition, dated January 1954, was in a single volume; the revised 2nd edition is more than twice as large. In addition to standard library references, a world-wide network of correspondents has kept the compiler supplied with up-to-date information. A vastly expanded edition of the *Handbook* is scheduled for publication by Advent under the title *The Encyclopedia of Science Fiction and Fantasy*; it will be in three hardbound volumes, the first to appear in 1973.

THE HERO-PULP INDEX, by Lohr McKinstry and Robert Weinberg. Second Edition. (Opar Press, Evergreen [Colo.], June 1971, [i] + 1-48 pp., octavo, offset, saddle-stapled in heavy paper covers, $5.00.)

This index lists the featured novel in each issue of 56 different "hero-pulp" magazines: Doc Savage, The Shadow, The Spider, Dusty Ayres, Tailspin Tommy, etc. Authors are identified, and the issues are cited by whole number, volume number, and cover date. There are separate checklists of authors, pen names, and reprints, as well as a 12-page "Guide to the Hero Pulps." In addition, there are full-page reproductions (in black and white) of 16 assorted pulp magazine covers.

There are a few minor errors, such as attributing all of the Captain Future novels bylined "Brett Sterling" to William Morrison, and neglecting to mention that "Morrison," in turn, is a pen name for Joseph Samachson, but these do not mar the usefulness of the compilation.

The first edition of this index was published by Robert Weinberg, Hillside [N.J.], May 1970, [i-iii] + 1-54 pp., quarto, offset, stapled in heavy paper covers, $5.00.

A HISTORY OF THE HUGO, NEBULA AND INTERNATIONAL FANTASY AWARD, LISTING NOMINEES AND WINNERS, 1951–1969, by Donald Franson and Howard DeVore (Sciencefiction Sales [DeVore], Dearborn Heights [Mich.], [1970], 1-45 pp., quarto, offset and mimeo, stapled in heavy paper covers, 50¢).

A brief history of the Hugo and International Fantasy Awards, with a complete list of nominees and winners through 1969, compiled by Donald Franson. Original publication data on all nominees is included. The corresponding coverage of the Nebula Awards (given by the Science Fiction Writers of America) was compiled by Howard DeVore.

THE IMAGINARY VOYAGE IN PROSE FICTION. A HISTORY OF ITS CRITICISM AND A GUIDE FOR ITS STUDY, WITH AN ANNOTATED CHECK LIST OF 215 IMAGINARY VOYAGES FROM 1700 TO 1800, by Philip Babcock Gove (Holland Press, London, 1961, vii-xi + 3-445 pp., octavo, boards, 63/- [$14.50]).

The checklist occupies pages 181-402. There is also a bibliography of books cited in the main text.

The first edition was published by Columbia University Press, 1941, $3.50.

AN INDEX TO NOVELS IN THE SCIENCE FICTION MAGAZINES, compiled by Gerry de la Ree (compiler, River Edge [N.J.], 1962, 1-19 pp., quarto, mimeo, stapled, $1.00). Edition limited to 100 copies.

The scope of this checklist is indicated by the title. The list was intended to aid science fiction readers in locating those magazine serials and book-length stories which had not yet been reprinted in book form. (Information supplied by Gerry de la Ree.)

THE INDEX TO THE SCIENCE-FANTASY PUBLISHERS, compiled and edited by Mark Owings and Jack L. Chalker (The Anthem Series, Baltimore [Md.], Aug. 1966, v-ix + 1-75 pp., quarto, mimeo, stapled in card covers, $5.00).

Limited numbered edition of approximately 300 copies. (A few copies were hard-bound and priced at $8.00.)

Subtitled: "A bibliography of the science fiction and fantasy specialty houses." The listing is restricted to thirty-six publishing houses which issued *only* sf, fantasy, or related nonfiction titles, and which produced at least one book in hardbound format. There is a capsule history of each imprint, and a detailed chronological bibliography of all titles published. The main listing is cross-indexed by author, title, and publisher.

This is a much-needed index, and the only one of its kind. Its usefulness is somewhat diminished by numerous small errors (regarding background history, dates, titles, pagination, dust-jacket artists, etc.). A revised and expanded edition has been promised.

NEW SF PUBLISHED IN GREAT BRITAIN: 1968, 1969, compiled by Gerald Bishop (Joanne Burger, Lake Jackson [Texas], 1970, 1-15 pp., quarto, hekto, stapled in paper covers, 35¢).

Science fiction and fantasy books published in Great Britain in 1968 and in 1969 are listed (in separate lists) by author only; there is no cross-index by title. For co-authored works, the entry appears under the first author's name, with no entry for the co-author. No distinction is made between new works and reprints.

"**The Science Fiction Book Index**," by Earl Kemp, in:
  The Best Science Fiction Stories and Novels: 1955, edited by T. E. Dikty (Frederick Fell, Inc., New York, 1955);
  The Best Science Fiction Stories and Novels: 1956, edited by T. E. Dikty (Frederick Fell, Inc., New York, 1956);
  The Best Science Fiction Stories and Novels: Ninth Series, edited by T. E. Dikty (Advent, Chicago, 1958).

Four lists, encompassing all English-language hardcover and paperback science fiction, fantasy, and related non-fiction for the calendar years 1954, 1955, 1956, and 1957. The 1954 and 1955 lists are in the two Frederick Fell volumes, while the remaining two lists are in the Advent volume.

Each anthology also contains an essay, "The Science Fiction Year," which surveys developments in the sf/fantasy field during the previous year. These essays are valuable critical and historical documents.

SCIENCE FICTION STORY INDEX 1950—1968, by Frederick Siemon (American Library Association, Chicago, 1971, x + 1-274 pp., printed, paper covers, $3.95).

The avowed purpose of this index is to list those science fiction stories published in anthologies and collections during the period 1950-1968. The publishers and the compiler preface this work with extravagant statements proclaiming its superiority over previous indexes. None of these claims is borne out by the work at hand. What it *does* make abundantly clear is that the compiler has little direct knowledge of science fiction, and apparently not much more of the science of bibliography. He has drawn his information from such sources as the *Cumulative Book Index*, and has apparently not bothered to check any of the data at first hand. How, otherwise, could he fail to distinguish between anthologies and single-author collections, or list novels as story collections, or omit literally hundreds of eligible books that were in print and widely available during the time this index was in preparation?

For extended analyses of the drawbacks of this work, we refer the reader to the review by Alexei Panshin in *Amazing Science Fiction Stories*, January 1972, and that by Randy Walters in *Luna Monthly*, October 1971.

SCIENCE FICTION TITLE CHANGES, by Michael Viggiano and Donald Franson (The National Fantasy Fan Federation, 1965, 47 pp., octavo, offset, $1.00).

Changing of titles when a book is reprinted is a widespread practice not only in the field of science fiction but in other areas of publishing as well. It is especially prevalent, and especially annoying, in the paperback field. The need for a compilation of title changes is obvious. The present listing would be more useful if it included full publishing data about the books listed. An up-dated and expanded edition is badly needed.

SF PUBLISHED IN 1968, compiled by Joanne Burger; 2nd edition (compiler, Lake Jackson [Texas], 29 March 1971, i-ii + 1-50 pp., quarto, mimeo, stapled in card covers, cover drawing by Patric Duvic, 75¢).

This is a listing of hardcover and paperback science fiction and fantasy books published in the U.S. in 1968. The main listing is by author, with a cross-index by title. Separate lists of nonfiction and juvenile books are included. Information on pen names, title changes, and series is provided. There are some errors (even in the corrected 2nd edition), some omissions, some non sf titles included by mistake, but these are minor defects and do not mar the usefulness of the compilation.

The first edition of this list was titled *Science Fiction Published in 1968* (compiler, Lake Jackson [Texas], Jan. 1969, i-ii + 1-50 pp., quarto, hekto, stapled in paper covers, 35¢).

SF PUBLISHED IN 1969, compiled by Joanne Burger; 2nd edition (compiler, Lake Jackson [Texas], 1971, 1-61 pp., quarto, mimeo, stapled in card covers, cover drawing by Alicia Austin, 75¢).

The alphabetical listing by author includes hardcover and paperback books, both fiction and non-fiction, giving full title, publisher, publisher's stock number (for paperbacks), price, and classification (collection, anthology, juvenile, etc.). The original title and copyright date of reprinted material are given in many cases. There is a cross-index by title, and separate lists of non-fiction, poetry and songs, and series stories. Typographical errors make some of the entries more mysterious than enlightening. There is no information on pen names.

The first edition of this checklist was published in June 1970, 2-55 pp., quarto, hekto, stapled in heavy paper covers, 75¢.

SF PUBLISHED IN 1970, compiled by Joanne Burger (compiler, Lake Jackson [Texas], 1971, i-ii + 1-48 pp., quarto, mimeo, stapled in card covers, cover drawing by Doug Potter III, 75¢).

Science fiction and fantasy books published in the U.S. in 1970 are listed by author and by title. There is a separate checklist of series stories. No information on pen names is included. No distinction is made between newly published books and reissues of earlier editions. There are some typographical errors (e.g., Marya Mannes' last name is transposed into "Nammes" and is consequently misplaced in the alphabetical listing).

This continuing series of annual indexes is of the utmost utility not only to readers and collectors of sf and fantasy, but to librarians and bibliographers. The compiler's evident intention to keep earlier editions in print in revised and corrected form is deserving of wholehearted support.

THE SUPPLEMENTAL CHECKLIST OF FANTASTIC LITERATURE, compiled by Bradford M. Day (Science-Fiction & Fantasy Publications, Denver [N.Y.], 1963, i-ii + 1-155 pp., quarto, mimeo, stapled in heavy card covers, no price given [$5.50]). Edition of 300 copies.

A compilation of English-language fantasy titles omitted from *The Checklist of Fantastic Literature* (q.v.) or published since the appearance of that book. Some of the information is incomplete (e.g., anthologies are not always identified as such), and typographical errors are frequent. Nonetheless, this is a useful work. Its scope is wider than that of the original *Checklist*. A number of plays and juvenile books are included.

THE TALE OF THE FUTURE, by I. F. Clarke, M.A. (The Library Association, London, 1961, 5-165 pp., octavo, boards, 20/-). Library

Association Bibliographies, No. 2 (sold for 15/- to Library Association members).

Full title and subtitle: *The Tale of the Future from the Beginning to the Present Day*. "A Check-list of those satires, ideal states, imaginary wars and invasions, political warnings and forecasts, interplanetary voyages and scientific romances—all located in an imaginary future period—that have been published in the United Kingdom between 1644 and 1960."

The book consists of a chronological list with annotations, together with cross-indexes by title and by author, a bibliography of sources, and five pages of Addenda.

The coverage of twentieth century material is a bit erratic. For example, some of Edgar Rice Burroughs' Pellucidar and Venus novels are listed, although they are definitely not "tales of the future." On the other hand, a number of titles by such familiar authors as Robert A. Heinlein, Edmond Hamilton, John Wyndham, and Raymond F. Jones are missing, although they existed in British editions prior to 1960. Many of the annotations are so brief and colorless as to convey no useful information: e.g., the description of Alfred Bester's pyrotechnic *Tiger! Tiger!* (U.S. title, *The Stars My Destination*) as merely "Adventures in the twenty-fourth century." There are also odd bits of misinformation regarding pseudonyms, such as the identification of Leigh Brackett (Mrs. Edmond Hamilton) as a *pen name* for Edmond Hamilton.

The data on pre-twentieth century material is valuable, and most of it has not been assembled in one place before.

THIRTY YEARS OF ARKHAM HOUSE, 1939—1969. A History and Bibliography, prepared by August Derleth (Arkham House, Sauk City [Wis.], 1960, 1-99 pp., octavo, boards, dust jacket design by Frank Utpatel, $3.50). Edition of 2000 copies.

An up-dating of *Arkham House: The First 20 Years* (q.v.), covering all books published through December 1969, and including a forecast of future titles. Pages 1-16 contain a brief history of Arkham House and associated imprints, and pages 19-99 contain the exhaustive bibliography. Illustrated with eight pages of photographs of Arkham House authors.

333: A BIBLIOGRAPHY OF THE SCIENCE-FANTASY NOVEL, by Joseph H. Crawford, Jr., James J. Donahue, and Donald M. Grant (The Grandon Company, Providence [R.I.], 1953, 1-80 pp., octavo, printed booklet, cover design by Roy Hunt, $1.50). Edition of 500 copies, of which 50 were hardbound.

Plot summaries of 333 selected sf and fantasy books (some of them rare and relatively unknown) published before 1951.

VOICES PROPHESYING WAR, 1763–1984, by I. F. Clarke (Oxford University Press, London, 1966, ix-x + 1-254 pp., octavo, boards, 32 illustrations, 42/-).

A scholarly yet lively survey of fiction centering around imaginary wars. Pages 227-249 contain a chronological checklist of fiction on this topic, from 1763 to 1965. Works in English, French and German are included. Other lists cover "Principal Works Consulted," "Select List of War Studies, 1770-1964," and an index of the works referred to in the text.

IV. Foreign Language Bibliographies

Note: The few titles listed here are only a sample of the large number of science fiction and fantasy bibliographies in languages other than English.

BEITRAEGE ZUR GESCHICHTE UND BIBLIOGRAPHIE DER UTOPISCHEN UND PHANTASTISCHEN LITERATUR, by Jakob Bleymehl (Offizin Bleymehl, Fürth/Saar, 1965, iv + 1-352 + 1-ix pp., paperbound).
Pages 1-81 contain a history and commentary on sf (interpreted broadly, so as to encompass utopian fiction, tales of marvellous voyages, etc.). Pages 85-125 contain a chronology of key works from 800 B.C. to 1948 A.D. Pages 129-346 are devoted to a bibliography of German-language sf. Pages 349-352 and i-ix contain appendices and addenda.

BIBLIOGRAFI OEVER SCIENCE FICTION OCH FANTASY 1772–1964, by Sam J. Lundwall (Fiktiva, Stockholm, 1964).
Second revised edition; first published in 1962.

INDEX TO *S-F MAGAZINE* [in Japanese], compiled by Fujio Ishihara; foreword by Masami Fukushima (Shambleau Press, Tokyo [?], Dec 1967, i + 9-316 pp., printed, paperbound).

An index to issues No. 1–100 (Feb 1960–Oct 1967) of the Japanese-language *S-F Magazine*. For those stories translated from English, the English-language title and original U.S. or British magazine publication are cited.

STORY INDEX Nr. I, 1955–1965, compiled by Alfred Vejchar (Austrotopia [Austria], Jan 1967, v-vi + viii + 1-78 + 1-18 pp.).

Part I (pages 1-78) contains a listing, arranged alphabetically by author, of short fiction published in German sf magazines and anthologies. Original sources of reprinted material are cited. Part II (pages 1-18) contains a listing of anthologies and series.

The booklet was published by Austrotopia, the Austrian sf fan organization.

TRANSGALAXIS: KATALOG DER DEUTSCHSPRACHIGEN UTOPISCH-PHANTASTISCHEN LITERATUR AUS FUENF JAHRHUNDERTEN (1460–1960), compiled by Heinz Bingenheimer (Transgalaxis [Schafer & Schmidt], Friederichsdorf/Ts. [West Germany], 1 Aug 1959, 7-123 pp., octavo, printed booklet, bound in paper covers). Edition of 5000 copies.

A bibliography, arranged alphabetically by author, of sf stories published in the German language. Translations from other languages are included. A separate list gives information about pseudonyms.

UTOPIE UND PHANTASTIK IM GEORG MUELLER VERLAG, by Roland Kloss ([compiler?], Berlin, 1966, unpaged, legal size, mimeo, bound in paper covers, no price given).

This is a list of the science fiction and fantasy books produced by the German publisher Georg Müller. The list is arranged alphabetically by author, and gives title, year of publication, and pagination for each entry.

Index

A. BOUCHER BIBLIOGRAPHY, 18
A. MERRITT: A BIBLIOGRAPHY OF FANTASTIC WRITINGS, 25
Ace Books, 30, 32
Adventure, 8
Air Wonder Stories, 4
Aldiss, Brian W., 13, 17
ALDOUS HUXLEY: A BIBLIOGRAPHY, 1916–1959, 23
All-American Fiction, 7
All-Story Magazine, 7
Amazing Stories, 5
Amazing Stories Annual, 5
Amazing Stories Quarterly, 5
Analog Science Fiction / Science Fact, 8
Anderson, Karen, 23
Anderson, Poul, 15, 17, 23
anthologies, 30, 31-32
Anthony, Piers: See Jacob, Piers A.
Argosy, The, 7
Arkham House, 21, 25, 29, 39
ARKHAM HOUSE: THE FIRST 20 YEARS, 1939–1959, 29
Armchair Detective, The, 18, 20
ARTHUR MACHEN: A BIBLIOGRAPHY, 25
Asimov, Isaac, 15
Astonishing Stories, 5, 6
Astounding Science Fiction, 1, 2, 5
Astounding Science Fiction (British), 8
Astounding Stories, 1, 2, 5
ASTOUNDING STORY-KEY, 1920–1951, 1
AUGUST DERLETH: TWENTY-FIVE YEARS OF WRITING, 21
Australian Science Fiction Association, 1, 8
AUSTRALIAN SCIENCE FICTION INDEX, 1925–1967, 1
AUTHENTIC SCIENCE FICTION, 2
AUTHOR'S WORKS LISTINGS, 15

Avon Books, 32
Avon Fantasy Reader, 9

Ballantine Books, 32
BEITRAEGE ZUR GESCHICHTE UND BIBLIOGRAPHIE DER UTOPISCHEN UND PHANTASTISCHEN LITERATUR, 41
Bell, Eric Temple: See Taine, John
Biamonti, Francesco, 22
BIBLIOGRAFI OEVER SCIENCE FICTION OCH FANTASY 1772–1964, 41
BIBLIOGRAPHY OF ADVENTURE, 16, 26
BIBLIOGRAPHY OF THE WORKS OF SIR HENRY RIDER HAGGARD, 1856–1925, A, 22
Bingenheimer, Heinz, 42
Bishop, Gerald, 2, 35
Bleiler, Everett F., 30
Bleymehl, Jakob, 41
Bloch, Robert, 12, 18, 23
Blue Book, 7
BLUEDEX/BLACKDEX, THE, 13
Boggs, D. W. [Redd], 1
Bond, Nelson S., 15
Boucher, Anthony, 18, 23
Bradbury, Ray, 18, 19, 23
Brennan, Joseph Payne, 24
Briney, R. E., 18, 20, 24
British Science Fiction Association, 4, 5, 13
BRITISH SCIENCE FICTION BOOK INDEX 1955, 29-30
Brown, Fredric, 15
Burger, Joanne, 35, 37-38
Burgess, Brian, 2, 5
Burroughs, Edgar Rice, 16, 19-20, 39

Campbell, John W., Jr., 16
Captain Future, 4, 5
Cavalier, The, 7
Chalker, Jack L., 24, 35
CHECKLIST OF ACE S-F THROUGH 1968, 30
CHECKLIST OF ANTHOLOGIES, A, 30
CHECKLIST OF *ASTOUNDING*, A, 2
CHECKLIST OF FANTASTIC LITERATURE, THE, 30-31, 38
CHECKLIST OF FANTASTIC LITERATURE IN PAPERBOUND BOOKS, THE, 31
CHECKLIST OF POUL ANDERSON, A, 17
CHECKLIST OF *SCIENCE FICTION ADVENTURES* (BRITISH EDITION), A, 2
CHECKLIST OF SCIENCE FICTION ANTHOLOGIES, A, 31-32
CHECKLIST OF SCIENCE FICTION, FANTASY, AND SUPERNATURAL STORIES AVAILABLE IN PAPERBACK IN BRITAIN, A, 32
CHECKLIST OF *VENTURE SCIENCE FICTION* MAGAZINE, A, 2
Christopher, J. R., 18
Clark, William J., 25
Clarke, Arthur C., 15
Clarke, I. F., 38, 40
Clement, Hal, 15
Cockcroft, T[homas] G. L., 9, 11, 24, 27
Cole, W[alter] R., 31
Comet, 5
COMPLETE CHECKLIST OF SCIENCE-FICTION MAGAZINES, THE, 3, 8
Complete Stories, 7
Cook, Frederick S., 4
Cosmic Stories, 6
Crawford, Joseph H., Jr., 40
Creasey, John, 20
Cummings, Ray, 15

INDEX

Danielson, Henry, 25
Dard, Roger, 4
Day, Bradford M., 3, 7, 16, 19, 25-26, 31, 38
Day, Donald B., 9, 10
de la Ree, Gerry, 35
Derleth, August, 4, 16, 21, 29, 39
DESTINY INDEX OF FANTASY–1953, THE, 3, 12
DeVore, Howard, 34
Dickensheet, D. W., 18
Donahue, James J., 40
DUKE UNIVERSITY UTOPIA COLLECTION, THE, 32
Durie, A. J. L., 9
Dynamic Science Fiction (British), 8
Dynamic Science Stories, 5

Eaton, J. Lloyd, 26
EDGAR RICE BURROUGHS: A BIBLIOGRAPHY, 19
EDWARD WOOD–EARL KEMP INDEX OF PAPERBOUND SCIENCE FANTASY, 1938-19–, THE, 32-33
Eerie Tales, 6
ELECTRIC BIBLIOGRAPH, Part 1, THE, 26
Electrical Experimenter, The, 3, 9
Engel, Theodore, 3
England, George Allan, 16
ERB-dom, 20
Eschelbach, Claire John, 23
Evans, William H., 5, 7-8, 24
Everybody's Magazine, 8
EVOLUTION OF MODERN SCIENCE FICTION, 3-4
Experimenter, The, 3, 9

F. and S. F. Book Co., ix
Famous Fantastic Mysteries, 5, 6
Fantast (Medway) Ltd., ix

Fantastic Adventures, 7
Fantastic Novels, 4, 5
FANTASTIC NOVELS: A CHECKLIST, 4
Fantastic Story Magazine, 4
Fantastic Story Quarterly, 4
Fantasy (British), 6, 8
Fantasy: The Magazine of Science Fiction, 6
Fantasy Commentator, 8
Fearn, John Russell, 21, 22
Fisher, Philip M., Jr., 16
Fitzgerald, William: See Leinster, Murray
Flint, Homer Eon, 16
Franson, Donald, 34, 37
FRED COOK'S INDEX TO THE WONDER GROUP, 4
From Unknown Worlds, 7
Future combined with Science Fiction, 6
Future Fiction (1st series), 5, 6
Future Fiction (British), 8
future wars, 38

GALAXY CHECKLIST, 4
Galaxy Magazine, 4
Galbreath, Robert, ix, 31
Gernsback, Hugo, 3-4
GOLDEN ANNIVERSARY BIBLIOGRAPHY OF EDGAR RICE BURROUGHS, A, 19
Golden Fleece, 6, 7, 11
Gove, Philip Babcock, 34
Grant, Donald M., 19, 40

H. G. WELLS: A COMPREHENSIVE BIBLIOGRAPHY, 27
H. P. LOVECRAFT: A BIBLIOGRAPHY, 24
Haggard, H. Rider, 16, 22
Hall, Austin, 16

Hall, Graham, 18
Hamilton, Edmond, 16
HANDBOOK OF SCIENCE FICTION AND FANTASY, A, 16, 33
Harbottle, Philip, 21, 22
Harrison, Harry, 22
HARRY HARRISON / BIBLIOGRAPHIA (1951–1965), 22
Harwood, John, 20
Heinlein, Robert A., 15
Heins, Henry Hardy, 19-20
HENRY KUTTNER. A MEMORIAL SYMPOSIUM, 23
HERO-PULP INDEX, THE, 33
HISTORY AND CHECKLIST OF *NEW WORLDS*, A, 5
HISTORY OF THE HUGO, NEBULA AND INTERNATIONAL FANTASY AWARD, 34
Hodgson, William Hope, 16
Hoffman, Stuart, 12
Howard Collector, The, 23
HOWARD PHILLIPS LOVECRAFT—MEMOIRS, CRITIQUES & BIBLIOGRAPHIES, 24
Howard, Robert E., 22-23
Hugo awards, 34
Huxley, Aldous, 23

Idler, The, 7
IMAGINARY VOYAGE IN PROSE FICTION, THE, 34
INDEX OF SCIENCE FICTION, 5
INDEX OF SCIENCE FICTION MAGAZINES, 1951–1965, THE, 5-6
[INDEX OF THE WORKS OF VARIOUS FANTASY AUTHORS, AN], 16
[INDEX OF VARIOUS FANTASY PUBLICATIONS, AN], 6
INDEX ON THE WEIRD & FANTASTICA IN MAGAZINES, AN, 3, 7-8

INDEX TO *ANALOG*, AN, 8
INDEX TO BRITISH SCIENCE FICTION MAGAZINES, 1934–1953, 8
INDEX TO FICTION IN *RADIO NEWS* AND OTHER MAGAZINES, 9
INDEX TO NOVELS IN THE SCIENCE FICTION MAGAZINES, AN, 35
INDEX TO *S-F MAGAZINE*, 42
INDEX TO THE BRITISH EDITIONS OF *THE MAGAZINE OF FANTASY AND SCIENCE FICTION*, AN, 9
INDEX TO THE SCIENCE-FANTASY PUBLISHERS, THE, 35
INDEX TO THE SCIENCE FICTION AND FANTASY MAGAZINES: 1963, 10
INDEX TO THE SCIENCE FICTION MAGAZINES, 1926–1950, 9-10
INDEX TO THE SCIENCE FICTION MAGAZINES [Al Lewis]: 1961, 10; 1962, 10
INDEX TO THE SCIENCE FICTION MAGAZINES [NESFA]: 1966, 10-11; 1967, 10-11; 1968, 11, 1969, 11; 1966-1970, 11
INDEX TO THE VERSE IN *WEIRD TALES*, 11
INDEX TO THE WEIRD FICTION MAGAZINES, 11-12
INDEX TO *UNKNOWN* AND *UNKNOWN WORLDS* BY AUTHOR AND BY TITLE, AN, 12
Ishihara, Fujio, 42
ITEM FORTY-THREE, 17

Jacob, Piers A., 10
Jakubowski, Maxim, 13
JDM MASTER CHECKLIST, THE, 25
Jeeves, B. T[erry], 2

INDEX

Jenkins, William Fitzgerald: See Leinster, Murray
JOHN CREASEY BIBLIOGRAPHY, A, 20
JOHN RUSSELL FEARN—AN EVALUATION, 20
JOHN RUSSELL FEARN: THE ULTIMATE ANALYSIS, 21
JOURNAL OF SCIENCE FICTION
  1951 MAGAZINE INDEX, 12
  1952 MAGAZINE INDEX, 12

Keller, David H., 15
Kemp, Earl, 3, 32, 36
Kline, Otis Adelbert, 15
Kloss, Roland, 42
Knight, Damon, 15
Kornbluth, Cyril M., 16
Kuttner, Henry, 18, 23

Laney, Francis T., 24
Leinster, Murray, 15, 23
Leman, Bob, 2
Lewis, Al, 10
Lewis, Anthony R., 10-11, 13
LITERATURE OF BURROUGHSIANA, THE, 20
Live Wire, 7
Long, Frank Belknap, 16
Lord, Glenn, 23
Lovecraft, H. P., 24
Lundwall, Sam J., 41

MacDonald, John D., 25
Machen, Arthur, 25
McKinstry, Lohr, 33
Magazine of Fantasy and Science Fiction, The, 19
Magazine of Fantasy and Science Fiction, The (British), 9

Magazine of Horror, 6
Magic Carpet, 7, 11
Manson, Margaret, 17
Marvel Science Stories, 5, 6
Marvel Stories, 6
Marvel Tales, 6, 7
Massoglia, Marty, 30
Merritt, Abraham, 16, 25
Meskys, Edmund R., 10
Metcalf, Norman, 5, 10
Miracle Science and Fantasy Stories, 5
MIT SCIENCE FICTION SOCIETY'S INDEX TO THE S-F MAGAZINES, 1951–1965, 11, 13
MITSFS, 10, 11, 13
Modern Electrics, 3, 9
Moffatt, Len and June, 25
Morse, A. Reynolds, 26
MULTI-MAN, THE, 22
Mundy, Talbot, 16, 25
Munsey, Frank A., 7
Munsey's Magazine, 7
MURRAY LEINSTER (WILL F. JENKINS): A BIBLIOGRAPHY, 23

National Fantasy Fan Federation, The, 6, 16
NEBULA, AN INDEX, 13
Nebula awards, 34
Negley, Glenn R., 32
New England Science Fiction Association, viii, 10-11
NEW H. P. LOVECRAFT BIBLIOGRAPHY, THE, 24
NEW SF PUBLISHED IN GREAT BRITAIN: 1968, 1969, 35
New Worlds, 5, 8
Nolan, William F., 18-19

Ocean, 7
100 BOOKS BY AUGUST DERLETH, 21

Oriental Stories, 7, 9, 11
Outlands, 6
Owings, Mark, 23, 26, 35

paperback sf/fantasy, 31, 32
Patten, Fred, 10
Peyton, Roger G., 2, 17
Planet Stories, 5
Popular Magazine, 7
Practical Electrics, 3, 9
publishers (science-fantasy), 35

Radio News, 3, 9
RAY BRADBURY INDEX, THE, 19
RAY BRADBURY REVIEW, 18-19
Red Star Adventures, 6
Reginald, Robert, 17
Richardson, Darrell C., 6, 16
Robbins, C. A. "Tod," 16
ROBERT BLOCH BIBLIOGRAPHY, 18
ROBERT E. HOWARD FANTASY BIBLIO, THE, 22-23
Rohmer, Sax, 16, 26, 31
Romance Magazine, 7
Russell, Eric Frank, 16

SAX ROHMER. A BIBLIOGRAPHY, 26
Schachner, Nathan, 15
Science and Invention, 3, 9
Science-Fantasy, 8
Science Fiction (1st series), 5, 6
Science Fiction (British), 8
Science Fiction Adventures (British), 2
"Science Fiction Book Index, The," 36
Science Fiction Quarterly (1st series), 5, 6
Science Fiction Quarterly (British), 8
SCIENCE FICTION STORY INDEX 1950–1968, 36

SCIENCE FICTION TITLE CHANGES, 37
Science Wonder Quarterly, 4
Science Wonder Stories, 4
Scoops, 5, 8
Scott, J. E., 22
Scrap Book, 7
SELECT BIBLIOGRAPHY OF H. P. LOVECRAFT, 24
S-F MAGAZINE [Japanese], 42
SF PUBLISHED IN 1968, 37
SF PUBLISHED IN 1969, 37-38
SF PUBLISHED IN 1970, 38
Shiel, M. P., 26
Shober, Joyce Lee, 23
Siemon, Frederick, 36
Simak, Clifford D., 16, 26
Slater, Kenneth F., 29, 32
Smith, Clark Ashton, 27
Space Stories, 4
Speer Decimal Classification, 5, 7
Startling Stories, 4, 5
STELLA NOVA, 17
Stevens, Francis, 16
Stirring Science Stories, 5, 6
Stone, Graham, 1
STORY INDEX Nr. I, 1955–1965, 42
Strange Stories, 7, 11
Strange Tales, 7, 9, 11, 16
Strange Tales (British), 8, 11
Strauss, Erwin S., 11, 13
Stribling, T. S., 16
Stubbs, Harry Clement: See Clement, Hal
Super Science Stories, 5
SUPPLEMENTAL CHECKLIST OF FANTASTIC LITERATURE, THE, 38

Taine, John, 16
TALBOT MUNDY BIBLIO, 25-26
TALE OF THE FUTURE, THE, 38-39

INDEX

TALES OF CLARK ASHTON SMITH, THE, 27
Tales of Magic and Mystery, 7
Tales of Wonder, 8
THIRTY YEARS OF ARKHAM HOUSE, 1939–1969, 39
333: A BIBLIOGRAPHY OF THE SCIENCE-FANTASY NOVEL, 40
Thrill Book, The, 7, 11
Thrilling Adventures, 8
Thrilling Stories, 8
Thrilling Wonder Stories, 4, 5
Top Notch, 8
Tracy, Louis, 26
TRANSGALAXIS, 42
Tuck, Donald H., 15, 23, 30, 33

Uncanny Stories, 5, 6
Unknown, Unknown Worlds, 7, 9, 12
Unusual Stories, 7
utopias, 32
UTOPIE UND PHANTASTIK IM GEORG MUELLER VERLAG, 42

Vejchar, Alfred, 42

Venture Science Fiction, 2
Viggiano, Michael, 37
VOICES PROPHESYING WAR, 1763–1984, 40

Weinbaum, Stanley G., 15, 16
Weinberg, Robert, 8, 22, 33-34
Weird Tales, 3, 6, 7, 9, 11, 12
WEIRD TALES INDEX, 7
Wells, H. G., 27
Wentz, W[alter] Jas., 25
Wetzel, George T., 24
Whitehead, Henry S., 15
Witch's Tales, The, 6, 7
Wonder Stories, 4, 5
Wonder Stories Annual, 4
Wonder Stories Quarterly, 4
Wood, Edward, 3, 12, 32
WORKS OF M. P. SHIEL, THE, 26
WSFA Journal, The, 23, 27

Yandro, 21

Zagat, Arthur Leo, 16